World Book's Learning Ladders
Weather

WORLD
BOOK

www.worldbook.com

World Book, Inc.
180 North LaSalle Street
Suite 900
Chicago, Illinois 60601
USA

For information about other World Book publications, visit our website at www.worldbook.com or call **1-800-WORLDBK (967-5325)**.

For information about sales to schools and libraries, call **1-800-975-3250 (United States)**; **1-800-837-5365 (Canada)**.

2008 revised printing

Library of Congress Cataloging-in-Publication Data

Weather.
    p. cm. -- (World Book's learning ladders)
    Summary: "Introduction to weather using simple text, question and answer format, illustrations, and photos. Features include puzzles and games, fun facts, a resource list, and an index"--Provided by publisher.
    Includes bibliographical references and index.
    ISBN 978-0-7166-7732-1
    1. Weather--Juvenile literature.   I. World Book, Inc.
QC981.3.W39 2008
551.6--dc22
                        2007018918

World Book's Learning Ladders
ISBN 978-0-7166-7725-3 (set, hc.)

Also available as:
ISBN 978-0-7166-7772-7 (e-book, Learning Hub)
ISBN 978-0-7166-7773-4 (e-book, Spindle)
ISBN 978-0-7166-7774-1 (e-book, EPUB3)
ISBN 978-0-7166-7775-8 (e-book, PDF)

Printed in China by Shenzhen Wing King Tong Paper Products Co, Ltd., Shenzhen, Guangdong
11th printing May 2017

Staff
Executive Committee
President: Jim O'Rourke
Vice President and Editor in Chief: Paul A. Kobasa
Vice President, Finance: Donald D. Keller
Vice President, Marketing: Jean Lin
Vice President, International Sales: Maksim Rutenberg
Director, Human Resources: Bev Ecker

Editorial
Director, Digital & Print Content Development: Emily Kline
Editor, Digital & Print Content Development: Kendra Muntz
Senior Editor: Shawn Brennan
Senior Editor: Dawn Krajcik
Manager, Indexing Services: David Pofelski
Manager, Contracts & Compliance (Rights & Permissions):
    Loranne K. Shields

Digital
Director, Digital Product Development: Erika Meller
Digital Product Manager: Jonathan Wills

Graphics and Design
Senior Art Director: Tom Evans
Coordinator, Design Development and Production: Brenda B. Tropinski

Manufacturing/Pre-Press
Manufacturing Manager: Anne Fritzinger
Proofreader: Nathalie Strassheim

This edition is an adaptation of the Ladders series published originally by T&N Children's Publishing, Inc., of Minnetonka, Minnesota.

Photographic credits: Cover: © Comstock/SuperStock; p4: Image Bank; p5: Tony Stone Images; p6: Tony Stone Images; p7: Telegraph Colour Library; p8: Tony Stone Images; p11: Tony Stone Images; p15: Still Pictures; p16: Two-Can Design; p17: Telegraph Colour Library; p18: Pictures Colour Library; p19: Retna; p20: Collections/Anthea Sieveking; p22 Tony Stone Images; p23: Bruce Coleman Ltd.

Illustrators: Fran Jordan, James Evans, Steve Holmes

What's inside?

This book tells you about different types of weather. You can find out how the weather changes during the year and what happens to plants and animals through the seasons.

Clouds and rain

Look up at the sky! Can you see any clouds? Are they white and fluffy or dark and gloomy? Clouds are made up of tiny drops of water. The drops grow bigger and heavier until they fall to the ground. It's raining!

This gray **cloud** is full of water and has just burst open!

Splish, splash! Lots of **raindrops** fall onto your hat.

When it pours rain, **puddles** of water are left on the ground.

Fog is a type of cloud that touches the ground. On a foggy day, it's hard to see far in front of you.

A **raincoat** keeps out the water. Inside, you stay cozy and dry.

This beautiful band of colors is called a rainbow. It appears when there is rain and sunshine at the same time.

This dog has **wet fur**, so it shakes itself dry. Watch out for the splashes!

Can you see the wavy **ripples** in the water?

Wind

You can't see the wind, but you can feel it on your skin. Sometimes, the wind feels warm, but at other times it's cold. These pictures show you what can happen on windy days.

A **gentle breeze** makes your socks and T-shirts flap about on the clothesline.

The wind is blowing hard enough to push this windsurfer across the choppy water.

Whoosh! In a **strong breeze**, these colorful kites soar high into the air.

Look out! A sudden **gust** of wind can turn your umbrella inside out!

A fierce wind called a tornado whirls around like a spinning top. It looks like a long funnel.

In a strong **gale**, the wind whistles through the trees. Leaves fly everywhere.

It's a fact!

A tornado can be so powerful that it can lift a mighty train high up into the air!

It's a storm!

When clouds in the sky loom big and dark, and the wind starts to howl, you know a storm is on the way. Suddenly, rain pours down. A storm can be exciting, but make sure you stay safely inside your home.

It's raining so hard that the road has started to **flood**.

A huge black **thundercloud** covers the sky.

Dazzling lightning is a giant spark of electricity from a thundercloud. It lights up the sky for a few seconds.

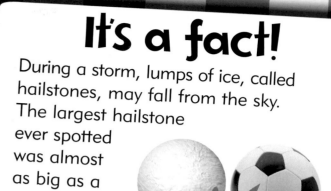

A flash of bright white **lightning** streaks through the sky.

Boom! If you see lightning, you will soon hear **thunder**.

9

Snow and ice

On a cold day, snow falls from the sky and covers the ground like a white carpet. You can make funny shapes out of fresh, wet snow. If it's freezing cold, the snow may turn into hard, slippery ice.

Water in the clouds freezes into white **snowflakes** that fall gently to the ground.

It's a fact!

In some of the coldest parts of the world, people called Inuit once built shelters called igloos out of snow and slabs of ice.

A smiling **snowman** lasts for as long as the weather stays cold.

The wind blows the snow into a big pile called a **snowdrift**.

Long, sharp **icicles** are frozen drips of water or snow.

It's fun to make **footprints** in the crunchy snow!

Look at this delicate, lacy snowflake. Each tiny flake of snow has a different pattern.

Family snapshots

Take a look at the vacation photographs in our album. People take vacations come rain or shine!

Words you know

Here are some words that you read earlier in this book. Say them out loud, then try to find the things in the pictures.

rainbow   raincoat

choppy water   puddles

thundercloud   snowflakes

Changing Seasons

Some places have four seasons called spring, summer, autumn, and winter. Each season brings its own kind of weather. As the weather warms up and cools down, look out for all kinds of changes that happen.

In spring, there are lots of **rain showers** and new flowers. The sun begins to shine more warmly, too.

spring

It's a fact!

When it's winter and chilly in the top half of the world, it's summer and sunny in the bottom half of the world!

In winter, it may start to **snow**. This is the coldest time of year.

winter

14

In summer, the **sun** is high in the sky and shines brightly. This is the hottest time of year.

Some countries have only two seasons, one dry and one rainy. In the rainy season, it can pour for months!

In autumn, some **leaves** change colors and the days turn cooler.

summer

autumn

Warm Spring

In spring, the weather warms up, and the days become longer. Now that the cold winter is over, plants push out of the ground and new leaves start to grow. Lots of baby animals are born, too.

Gardeners are busy at this time of year. Gentle rain and warm sunshine help young plants to grow quickly.

Hundreds of tiny **buds** start to unfold.

The buds become bright green **new leaves**.

Spring is a colorful season. The first **flowers** start to bloom.

A **baby lamb** has a thick woolen coat to keep it warm on cooler days.

A bird has returned from its winter home far away. It has built a snug **nest**.

The bird lays **eggs** in the nest. The eggs will hatch late in the spring.

These fluffy ducklings are a few weeks old. There is plenty of food to eat, so soon they will be big and strong.

Hot summer

In summer, the days are long and warm. It's fun to play outside when the sun shines brightly and the sky is blue. Insects buzz and flutter around gardens, which are packed with colorful, scented flowers.

The warm golden **sunshine** helps the flowers bloom.

Splashing in the **water** is a fun way to keep cool.

A striped bee lands on a flower. The bee collects a sweet juice called nectar.

A **sun hat** and sunglasses protect you from the sun's hot rays.

Make sure you rub plenty of sun block into your skin. It will help protect your skin from the strong sunshine.

The cat looks comfortable resting in the cool **shade**.

Bright **butterflies** flutter through the garden.

19

Cool autumn

On an autumn day, it's fresh and cool, even when the sun shines. Trees lose their leaves, fruit ripens, and animals prepare for the cold winter months. Early in the morning, the air may feel damp.

Colorful leaves fall from branches.

It's fun to **rake** the leaves that have fallen from the tree.

Juicy red apples are ready to be picked from the tree. This apple tastes sweet!

A **squirrel** collects nuts. It stores them, then eats them during the cold winter.

There are tasty **nuts** for animals to eat.

These **birds** are about to fly to a warmer place far away. They'll return in the spring.

It's a fact!

A squirrel hides nuts for the winter in all kinds of nooks and crannies, but sometimes it forgets where it has put them!

Cold winter

In winter, days are short, and nights are long. The sun's rays are weak, and the weather turns cold. Many animals hide until the warm spring. Others are up and about during the cold weather.

There are many **bare trees** in winter. The leaves fell off the trees in autumn.

This plant is covered in a coat of frost. It looks like icing on a cake!

It's so cold that the water in this pond has frozen into **ice**.

Even in freezing winter, **pine trees** keep their leaves, called needles.

There's little food for birds to eat, except winter **berries**.

In the cold winter months, a dormouse sleeps in a cozy nest. It won't wake up until the warm spring arrives.

23

Seasons projects

Look at these colorful projects. They're perfect for keeping a record of changes through the seasons.

spring

summer

autumn

winter

Words you know

Here are some words that you read earlier in this book. Say them out loud, then try to find the things in the pictures.

bare trees	butterflies
nuts	berries
lambs	flowers

How many fluttering butterflies can you count?

25

Did you know?

The bands of color in a rainbow always appear in the same order: red, orange, yellow, green, blue, indigo, and violet.

About 600 bolts of lightning strike the Earth every minute.

You can tell how far away a thunderstorm is. Every 4 seconds between a lightning flash and a thunderclap counts as 1 mile (1.6 kilometers) away.

Research shows that windy, stormy weather often makes people grumpy!

Most of the world's tornadoes happen in an area called "Tornado Alley" that stretches across the Midwestern and Southern United States.

A raindrop may contain about 1 million cloud droplets before it is heavy enough to fall.

Puzzles

Close-up!

We've zoomed in on different kinds of weather. Can you guess what is in each picture?

1

2

3

Answers on page 32.

Double trouble!

Look at these two pictures of a rainy day. Can you find four differences between picture a and picture b?

a

b

Match up!

Match each word on the left with its picture on the right.

a

1. cloud

b

2. rainbow

c

3. tornado

d

4. lightning

e

5. snowflake

6. hailstone

f

Answers on page 32.

True or false

Can you figure out which of these statements are true? You can go to the page numbers listed to help you find out the answers.

A tornado can be so powerful that it can lift a train into the air. **Go to page 7.**

3

In the rainiest place in the world, enough rain falls yearly to cover a three-story building. **Go to page 5.**

1

When it's winter in the top half of the world, it's summer in the bottom half. **Go to page 14.**

4

2 Some hailstones are as big as beach balls. **Go to page 9.**

A squirrel always remembers where it has hidden its nuts. **Go to page 21.**

5

Answers on page 32.

Find out more

Books

How Does the Wind Blow? Patricia J. Murphy (Benchmark Books, 2007)
Charts, pictures, and a fun activity help answer your questions about the wind.

How's the Weather? Martha E. H. Rustad (Capstone Press, 2006) 6 volumes
Each book in this set examines one of six types of weather days: cold, hot, rainy, snowy, sunny, and windy.

Scholastic News Nonfiction Readers: Weather, Katie Marisco and Pam Rosenberg (Children's Press, 2007) 6 volumes
How does a rainy weather day affect what you do? Or a snowy day? Or a sunny day? Find out in one of these six books.

Storms! Leslie Dickstein (HarperCollins, 2006)
In magazine style, this book helps you understand stormy weather.

Why Does It Rain? Judith Jango-Cohen (Millbrook Press, 2006)
Learn about Earth's water cycle, from water to water vapor to rain and back to water.

Websites

Dan's Wild Wild Weather Page, Dan Satterfield
http://www.wildwildweather.com
Dan, a TV weatherman, offers his knowledge about all kinds of weather events, tells how to do your own forecasting, gives a tour of his forecast office, and provides games and puzzles related to weather.

FEMA for Kids: For the Little Ones, Federal Emergency Management Agency
http://www.ready.gov/kids/fun-games
A coloring book, stories, photos, and advice on how to prepare for weather disasters are some features of this government website.

Owlie Skywarn's Weather Book, National Weather Service
http://nws.noaa.gov/om/brochures/OwlieSkywarnBrochure.pdf
Learn to recognize dangerous weather and follow Owlie's safety warnings.

The Storm, wcm Solutions
http://www.wcmsolutions.com/products/thestorm/index.html
Press the button and create your own thunderstorm, lightning and all!

Weather Wiz Kids, The Indy Channel
http://weatherwizkids.com
Enjoy weather folklore, games, and jokes as you also learn the facts about the wind and clouds, hurricanes and tornadoes, and other weather features.

Answers

Puzzles
from pages 28 and 29

Close-up!
1. sun
2. icicles
3. raindrops

Double trouble!
In picture b, the rainbow, splashes, and one puddle are missing; the boots are purple.

Match up!
1. e
2. c
3. a
4. f
5. b
6. d

True or false
from page 30

1. true
2. false
3. true
4. true
5. false

Index